Trademarks
coloring book

David Sorkin

TRADEMARKS COLORING BOOK

The trademarks and service marks depicted in this book are the property of their respective owners. Most or all are the subject of registrations with the United States Patent and Trademark Office. Interested readers may find further information about trademarks at the USPTO's website, www.uspto.gov.

Coca-Cola is among the best-known brands in the world. The company's instantly recognizable marks include Coca-Cola and its distinctive bottle shape.

The Quaker Man was the first registered trademark for a breakfast cereal.

Don't mess with Texas®

"Don't mess with Texas" was originally an anti-littering slogan.

Mountain Dew has changed its logo quite a bit over the years.

McDonald's is another world-famous mark. Its early restaurants included real arches as a design feature. The arches were eventually incorporated into the company's logo.

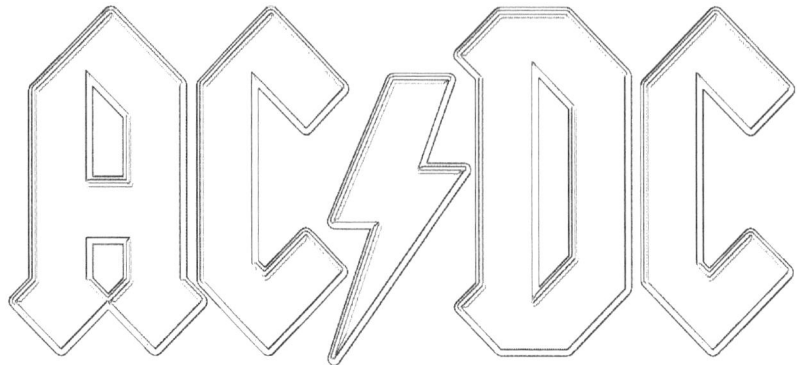

Band logos: AC-DC, Aerosmith, The Beatles

Cheerios

PEP O MINT LIFE SAVERS

SPAGHETTIOS

Oh, I see it!
Each of these marks includes a picture of the product.

EBay updated its logo in 2012, retaining the same basic color scheme but dropping the misaligned lettering.

Google changed its logo in 2015, keeping the same colors but shifting to
a sans-serif font for improved readability on small screens.

More band logos: Cheap Trick, Def Leppard, The Doors

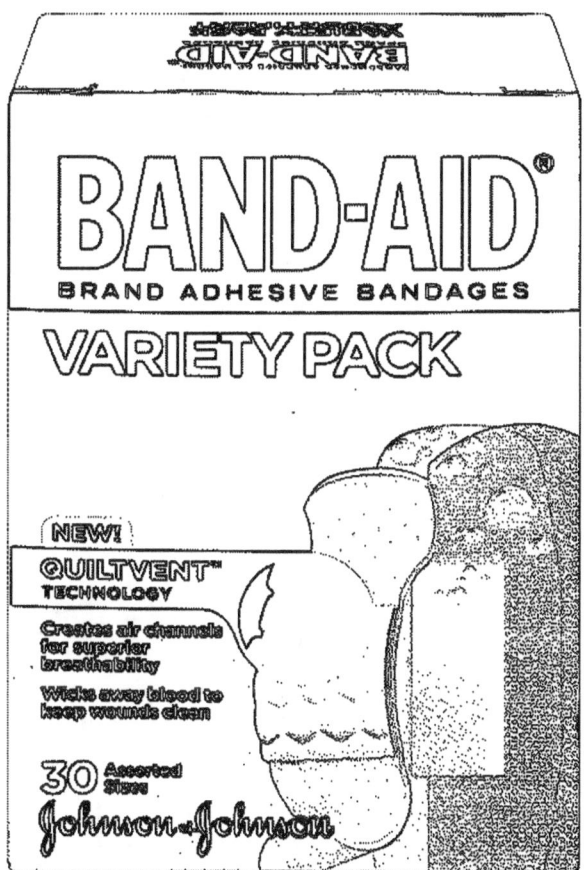

The packaging may have changed over the years,
but Band-Aid's trademark hasn't.

amazon

These marks are designed to make you smile.

Major League Baseball, the National Basketball Association, and the
National Football League all have red-white-and-blue logos.

Apple's rainbow of colors has given way to a simple silhouette.

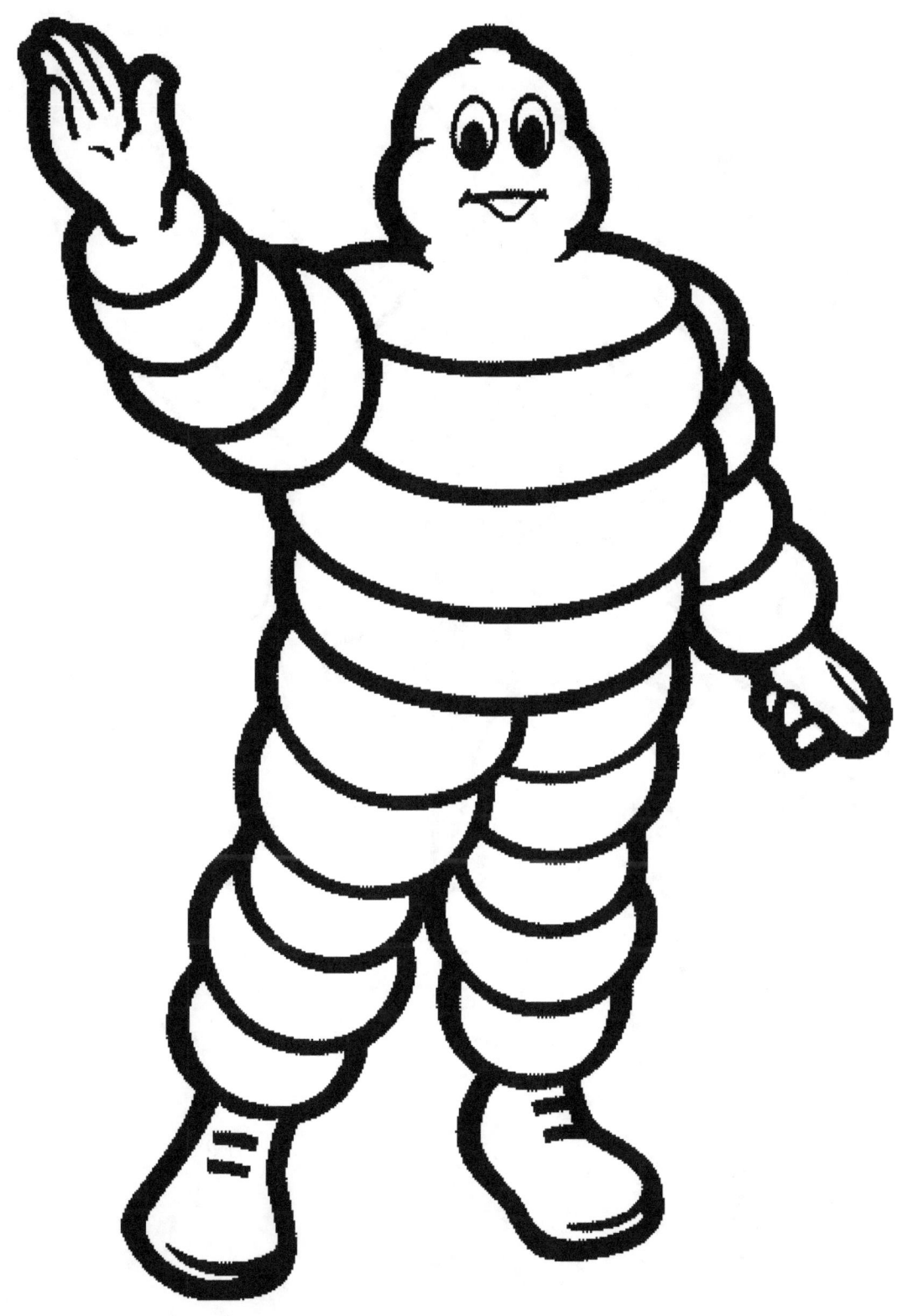

It's hard not to wonder if the Pillsbury Dough Boy
is related to the Michelin Man.

This was the Morton Salt girl back in 1956.

And here she is today. When it rains, it pours!

More band logos: Fall Out Boy, Grateful Dead, Kiss, Led Zeppelin

Spam hasn't changed much over the years.

Look closely, and you'll see the word "Mom" hidden in the new Wendy's logo.

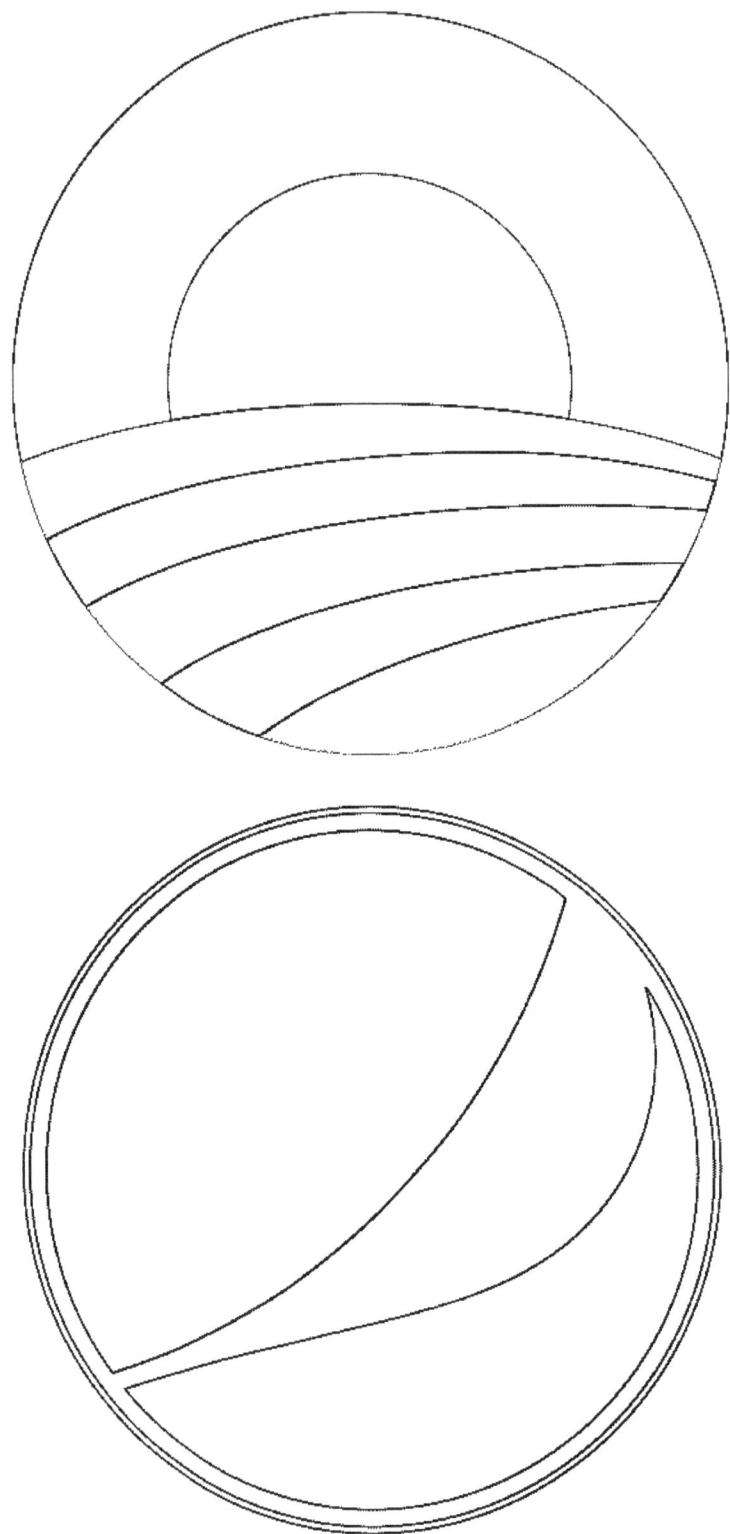

Some people think that the Pepsi logo looks like Barack Obama's campaign logo. Other people think that the Obama logo looks like Donald Trump if you turn it upside down.

There's a cup of coffee in the Dunkin' Donuts logo,
and a hamburger in Burger King's.

More band logos: Metallica, Rolling Stones, Van Halen

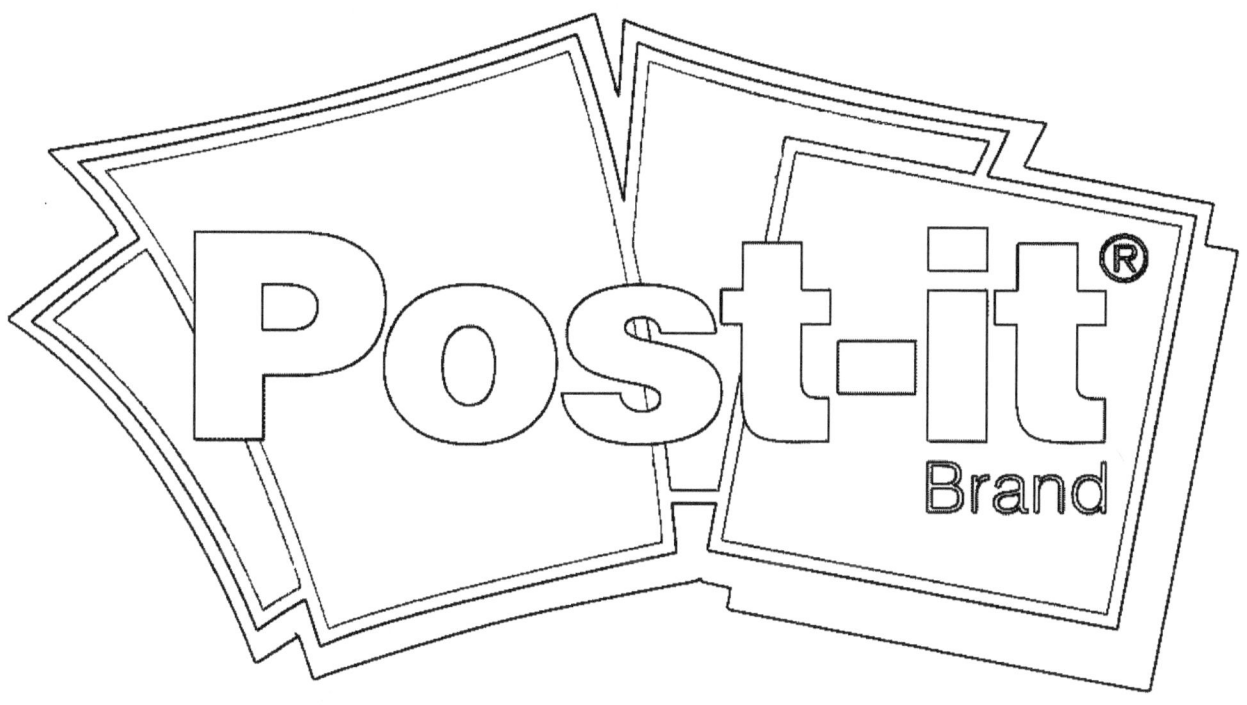

"Post-it" is 3M's trademark for its repositionable
sticky notes and related products.

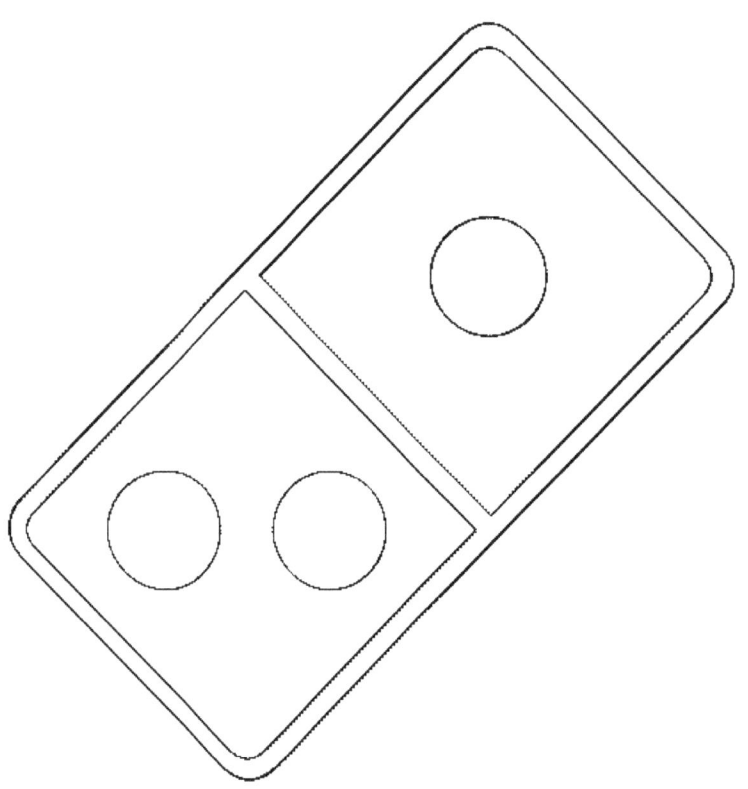

For those who like their logos literal: a bell, a domino, and a castle.

Colonel Sanders is still there, but Kentucky Fried Chicken is now just KFC.

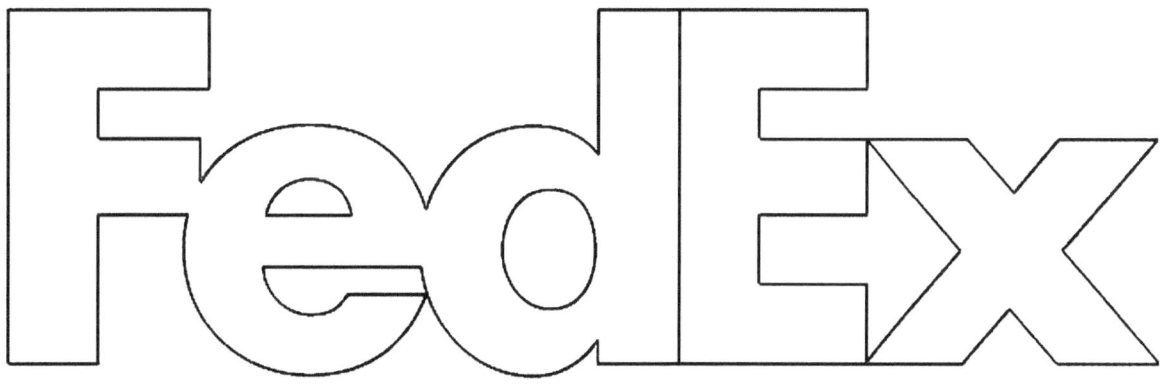

FedEx's logo includes an arrow created by the negative space between letters.

Baskin Robbins also has a hidden component in its logo—the number 31,
a reference to the company's "31 flavors" slogan.

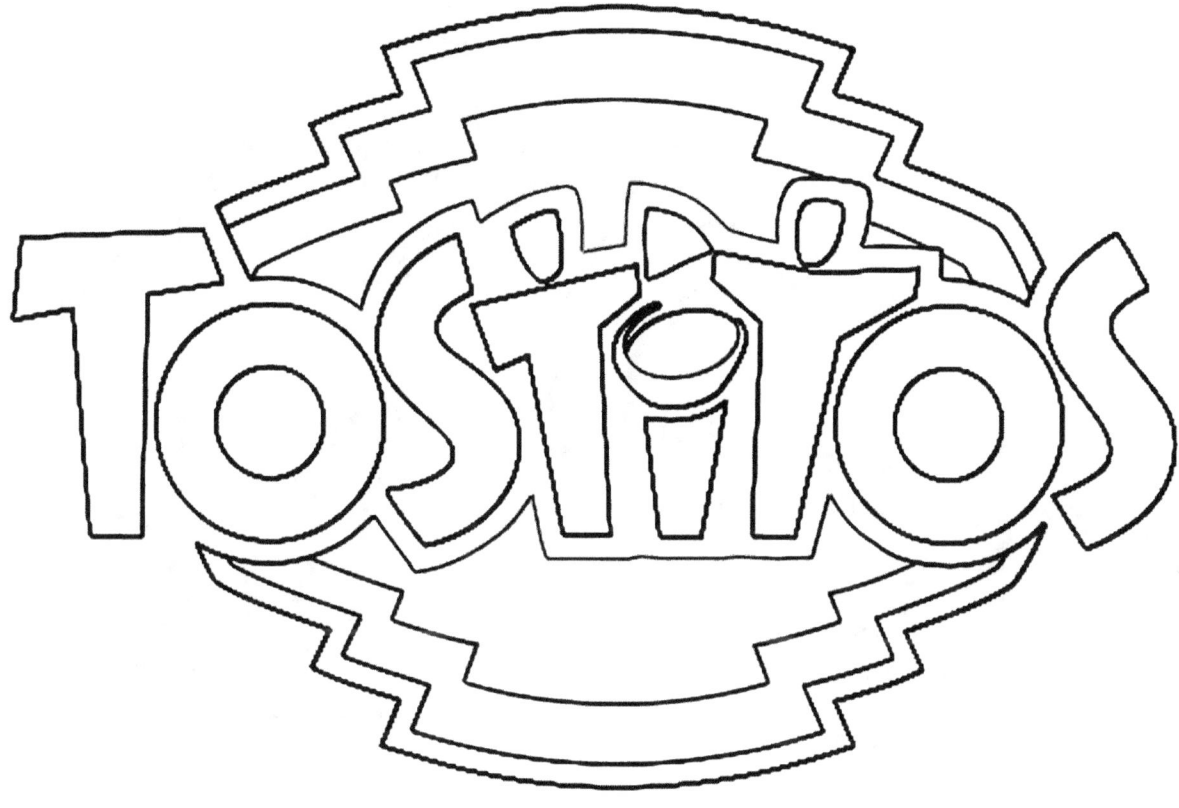

Here's another one with a hidden component—two people
holding a giant tortilla chip over a bowl of salsa.

RCA has used several variations of this logo over the years, illustrating the company's slogan "His Master's Voice." The original version featured an Edison Bell cylinder phonograph. Nipper, the dog that modeled for the logo, was probably part Jack Russell Terrier.

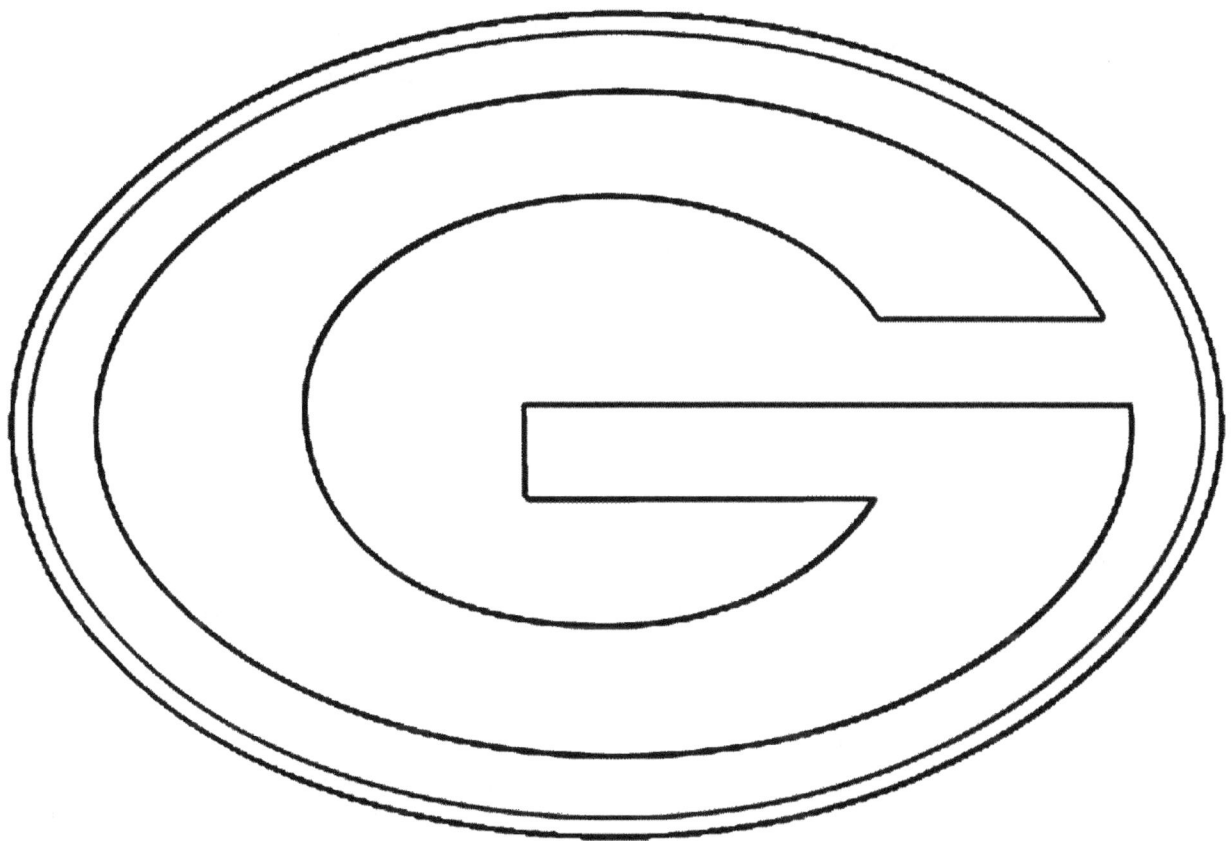

Grambling State and the University of Georgia are
among the teams that have adopted this "G" logo.

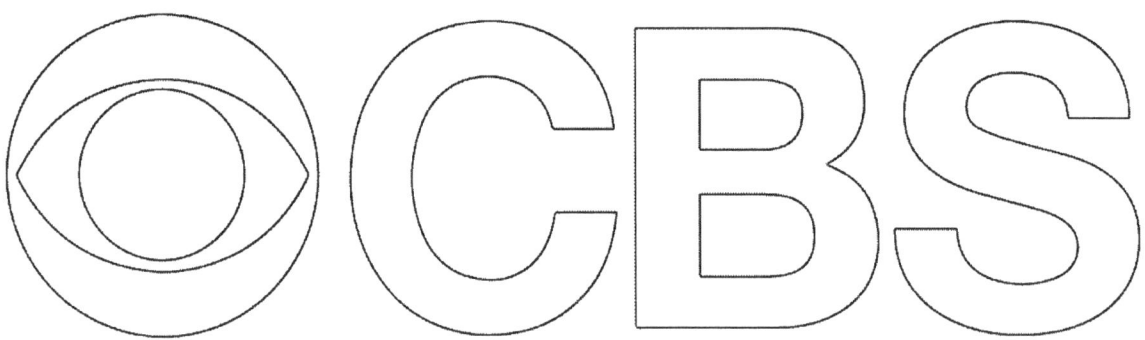

ABC's logo hasn't changed much since the early 1960s.
The CBS Eye has been around in various forms since 1951.

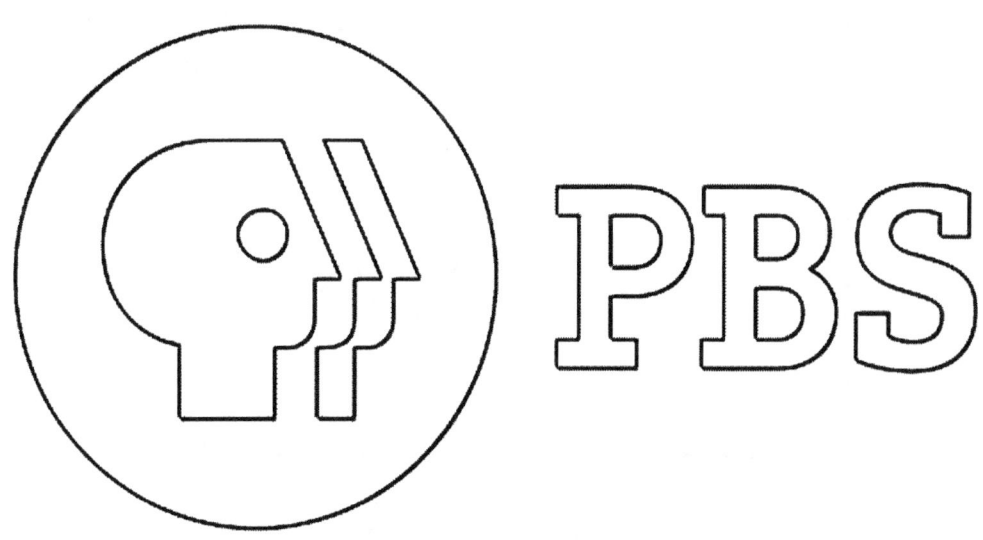

NBC uses negative space to embed the network's iconic peacock.
The PBS logo retains the "P-head" from earlier incarnations.

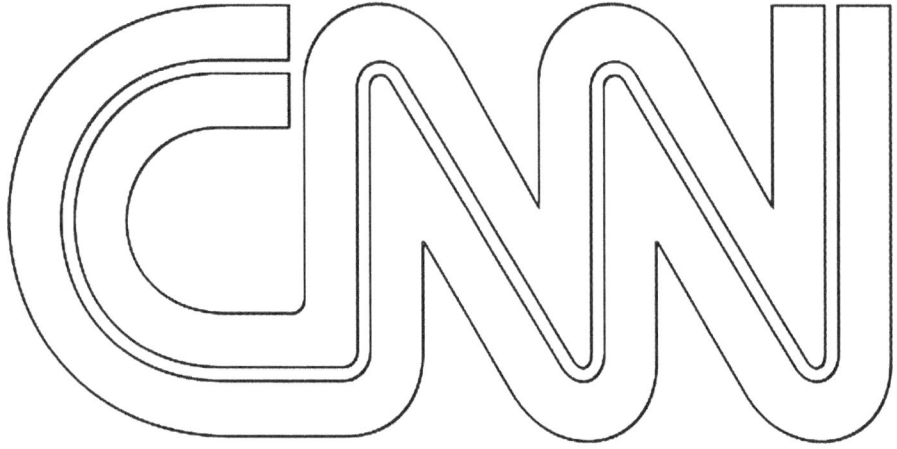

CNN and MTV are among the most popular cable channels,
and both have widely recognized logos.

Coincidence? There's a striking similarity between the logos of
Columbia Sportswear and Sun Microsystems (now part of Oracle).

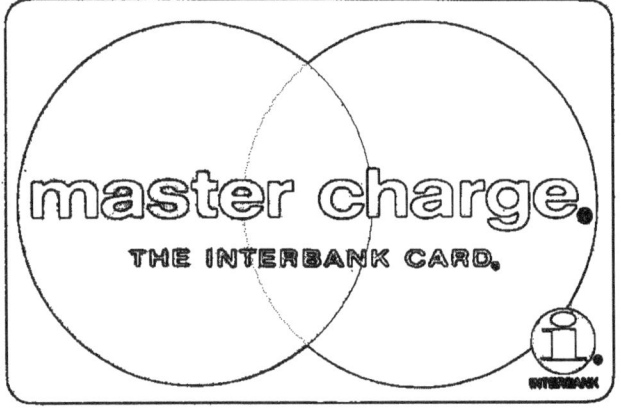
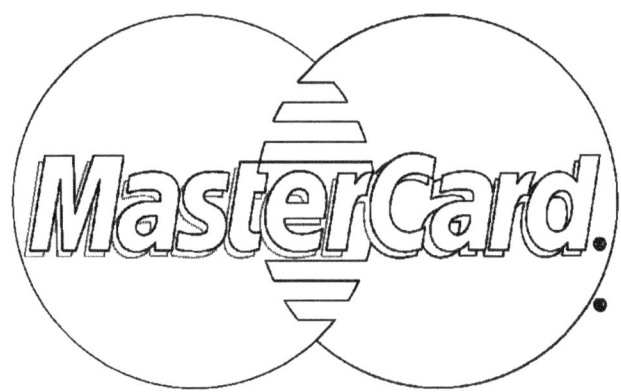

MasterCard and Visa have evolved over the years.

Only YOU can prevent forest fires.

44

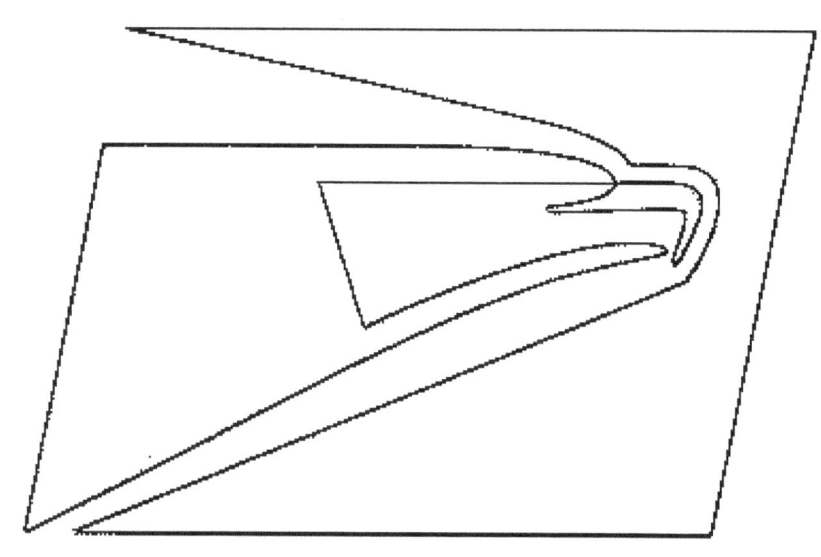

Mr. ZIP debuted in the early 1960s to promote the use of ZIP codes.

The Boston Celtics logo was designed by Zang Auerbach,
the brother of legendary coach Red Auerbach.

Notre Dame's leprechaun prepares for a pummeling from Purdue Pete.

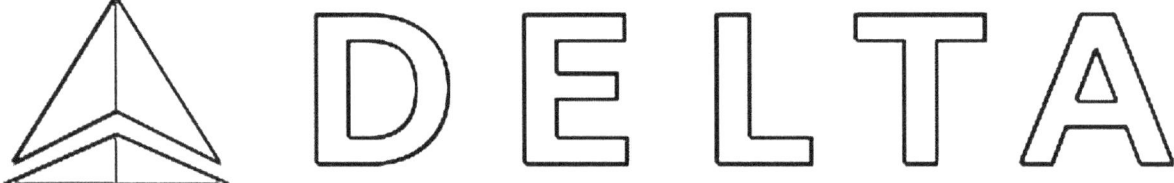

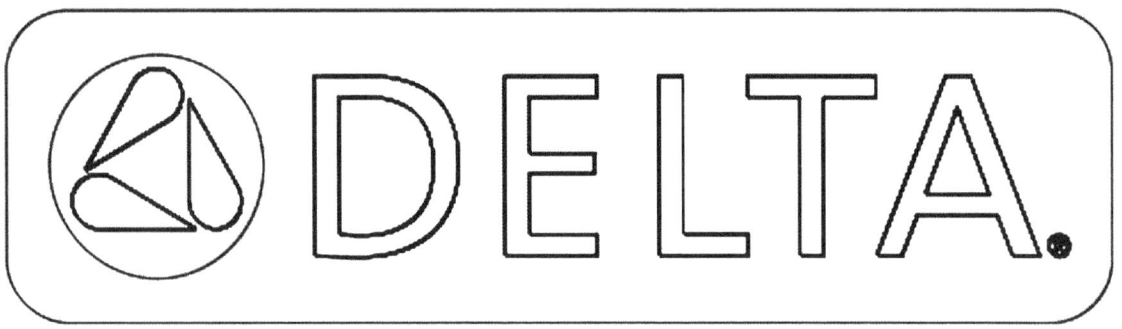

Delta Air Lines and Delta Faucet are unrelated
companies with remarkably similar logos.

Yes, you can buy Tide at Target.

Oops.

Fruit of the Loom has been around since the mid-19th century. It is among
the world's oldest brands—its trademark was first registered in 1871.

Dreyer's ice cream is marketed under the Edy's mark in the Eastern and Midwestern United States, to avoid confusion with Breyers.

Geek Squad is a subsidiary of big-box electronics retailer Best Buy.

Baby Ruth's manufacturer claimed that the candy bar was named after Ruth Cleveland, daughter of President Grover Cleveland, rather than famous baseball player Herman "Babe" Ruth.

Even if you're partial to Cheese Nips, you do have to
appreciate the cracker in the Cheez-It logo.

56

Holiday Inn phased out its "Great Sign" in the early 1980s.

Sorry, Charlie. It's tuna, not chicken.

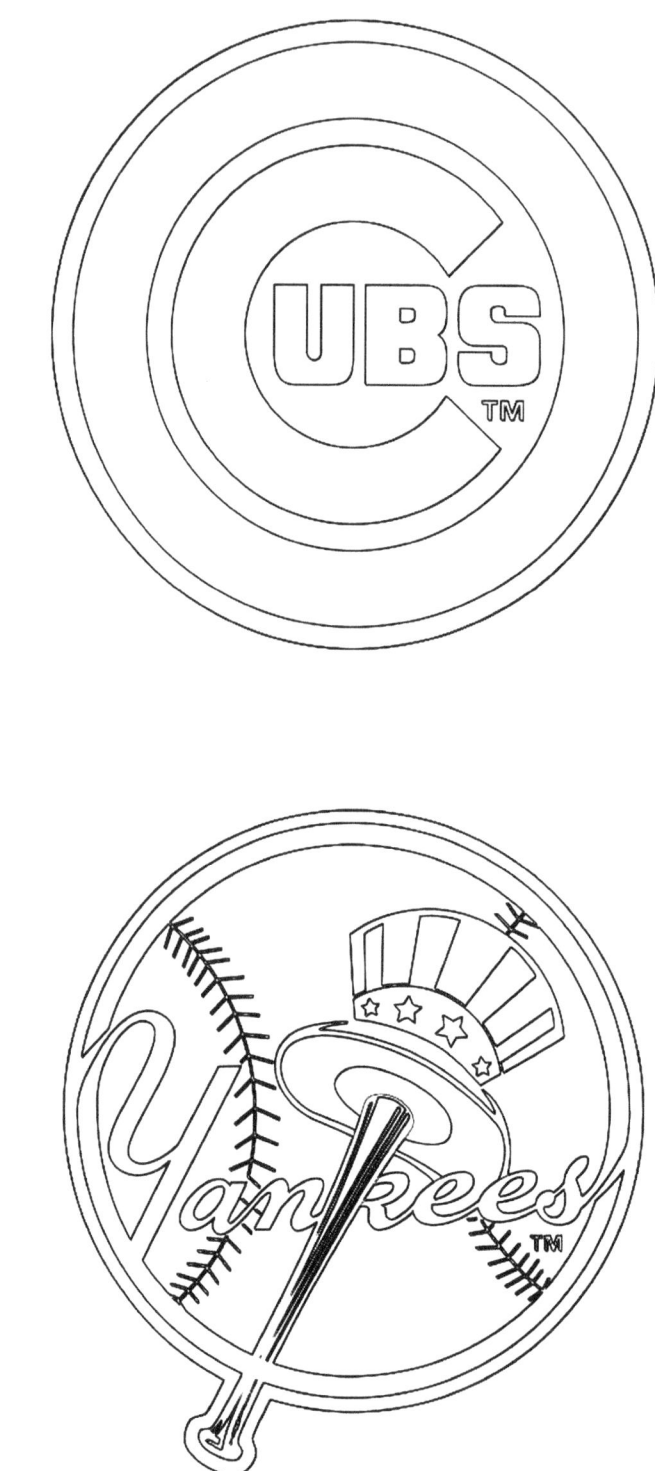

The New York Yankees have won 27 World Series championships.